Acknowledgments

This book couldn't have been possible without the dedicated support from the following team of cats:

Spud:
Editor in Whiskers
A tuxedo cat with a love for food, cuddles, and sitting in puddles. He contributed much of the 'crazy' to this book, constantly raising the bar and demanding more from potential Crazy Cat Ladies.

Harry:
Quality Control
A ginger cat known for making sure everyone behaves as they should, he can exert some quality control over his colleague and best friend Spud's wilder attempts by distracting him with catnip and cheese treats.

Acknowledgments

Spotti-Dotti:
Lead Researcher
A meticulous tuxedo cat who is suspicious of everything and everyone, especially Spud and Harry. Her ability to correct their factual mistakes and tidy up after them is both key to this book and ensuring the kitchen is spotless after dinner.

Ruffi-Tuffi:
Delivery Girl
A small calico cat who wears her 'runt of the litter' badge with pride. Ruffi-Tuffi will personally deliver each book in her small backpack. She appreciates her tips in the form of treats.

Dandelion Heart (aka Dandy, aka Horribilly):
Food Tester
The youngest of all our helpers, Dandy is a ginger cat who – with great dedication - tested all food suggestions that ended up in this book. He especially recommends the salmon bites.

Gracie:
Gracie [note from Harry: not an editing error]
Gracie is the last of the three tuxedo cats, and she contributed nothing to the book other than sitting around looking pretty. We couldn't have done this without her.

YOU KNOW YOU'RE A CRAZY CAT LADY IF...

FIND OUT HOW OBSESSED YOU ARE!

HEIDI BEE

© 2022 HEIDI BEE.

PLEASE DO NOT REPRODUCE
WITHOUT PERMISSION.

ALL INQUIRIES CAN BE SENT TO:
HEIDIBEEPUBLISHING@GMAIL.COM

Welcome!

Cats have an extraordinary ability to capture our hearts and souls with their charming antics, purring melodies, and irresistibly cute faces. For some humans, this enchantment deepens into a lifelong passion — a devotion that transforms them into something unique, something special, something affectionately known as a "crazy cat lady."

"You Know You're a Crazy Cat Lady If... Find Out How Obsessed You Are!" is your delightful guide to exploring the fascinating world of cat lovers, revealing the quirks, idiosyncrasies, and sheer joy of embracing your feline friends wholeheartedly.

Welcome!

Whether you're already proudly wearing the title of a "crazy cat lady" or teetering on the edge of cat-induced madness, this book is your ticket to understanding, embracing, and even celebrating your unique cat-loving persona.

Within these pages, you'll embark on a journey of self-discovery, discovering just how deep your love for cats runs. From your unparalleled talent for deciphering your cat's every meow to your uncanny ability to turn every piece of furniture into a scratching post, each section will unveil the distinctive traits and behaviors that set you apart as a true cat aficionado.

You'll giggle, nod knowingly, and maybe even blush a little as you recognize yourself in these pages.

Are you a proud parent to multiple cats, each with their own elaborate backstories? Do you find yourself spending more on cat toys and treats than on your own indulgences? Have you mastered the art of interpreting the feline gaze and learned to appreciate a hearty cat hair garnish on every outfit? If you answered "yes" to any of these questions, then congratulations, you might just be a bona fide crazy cat lady!

Welcome!

So, grab your coziest blanket, curl up with your favorite feline companions, and embark on a journey through this light-hearted exploration of all things cat-related. Whether you're looking for validation, a sense of community, or just a good laugh, "You Know You're a Crazy Cat Lady If..." promises to be the purr-fect companion for every cat enthusiast. Let the adventure begin!

Part 1: Are YOU a Crazy Cat Lady?

Our first quiz examines whether you meet the lofty criteria of a Crazy Cat Lady as set by our Editor in Whiskers, Spud. Before we start, however, our Cat Historian, Spotti Dotti, has some information about how the concept of the 'crazy cat lady' came about.

The History of Crazy Cat Ladies
The term "crazy cat lady" has become a popular way to describe women with many cats who are often portrayed as eccentric or eccentrically obsessed with their feline companions. This stereotype has deep historical roots and has evolved into a cultural phenomenon.

Ancient Egypt: Cats as Sacred Companions

The history of the "crazy cat lady" can be traced back to ancient Egypt, where cats were held in high esteem. Cats were considered sacred animals and were often associated with the goddess Bastet, who had a feline appearance. In ancient Egyptian society, women were often depicted with cats in art, reflecting the close relationship between women and their feline companions.

Middle Ages: Cats and the Witch Hunts

The perception of women who kept cats shifted in the Middle Ages. During the witch hunts of the 16th and 17th centuries, many women were accused of witchcraft, and their cats were often considered their familiar spirits. The association between women, cats, and witchcraft led to negative stereotypes, painting women who owned many cats as suspicious or eccentric.

Victorian Era: The Beginnings of Cat Hoarding

In the 19th century, with the rise of the Victorian era, the image of the "crazy cat lady" began to truly take shape. Victorian society was fascinated with animals and saw them as objects of curiosity and companionship. However, some women's obsession with cats started to border on hoarding, collecting an excessive number of them.

The term "cat lady" was coined during this time, reflecting the growing social awareness of this phenomenon.

20th Century: The Pop Culture Emergence

The image of the "crazy cat lady" further solidified in the 20th century, with popular culture depicting women with numerous cats as lonely, eccentric, and obsessed. This portrayal can be seen in literature, films, and television, where cat ladies became recurring characters or stereotypes. A prime example is the character Eleanor Abernathy, the "Crazy Cat Lady" from the long-running TV show The Simpsons.

Modern Times: The Internet and Cat Memes

In the digital age, the "crazy cat lady" stereotype has found new life online. Cat memes, social media, and viral videos have only perpetuated the image of women who adore cats as peculiar or "crazy." While many people share their love for cats online, the stereotype endures, often in a playful or self-deprecating manner.

Changing Perceptions: Cat Rescue and Advocacy

In recent years, there has been a shift in how society views 'crazy cat ladies.' Instead of being perceived solely as a gendered stereotype, the term has come to warmly encompass people of all genders and cat-loving persuasions. The title has been claimed back by the many crazy cat ladies of the world, who have rewritten the rules on what being cat mad really is: dedicated, loving, committed. Many crazy cat ladies are now recognized for being involved in cat rescue and advocacy or celebrated for their humor and creativity. While a bit of madness itself may remain an important part of who we are, it is madness we now choose for ourselves in a mindful and loving way.

Now, onto the first quiz, which will determine if you really *are* a crazy cat lady!

Each question will have four possible answers. Circle the one that fits you best, then add up how many of each letter you scored.

How many cat-related shirts do you own?
a) None. Cats and fashion don't mix.
b) Just one. I like to show my love occasionally.
c) Enough to open a cat-themed boutique.
d) I lost count, but I'm wearing one right now!

What's your typical reaction when you see a cute cat video?
a) I don't tend to watch cat videos.
b) I might watch it and go "aww" for a second.
c) I watch it, share it with my friends, and then watch it again!
d) I've watched so many that I've become immune to their cuteness.

What does your home decor consist of?
a) Neutral colors with no cat references.
b) A cat-themed trinket here and there.
c) Multiple cat figurines, cat art, or cat-shaped pillows.
d) My home is basically a cat museum.

All I want for Christmas is …
a) You!
b) A cute pair of cat earrings.
c) A photo book filled with adorable pictures of my cats.
d) An all-expenses paid holiday for me and my cat – we deserve it!

What do you do when you see a stray cat?
a) Keep walking. Strays make me a little nervous.
b) Stop and pet it if it seems friendly.
c) Stay for several minutes to chat with it.
d) I scoop it up and take it home, even if it's against my better judgment.

How many cat-related puns can you come up with?
a) Puns? I'm not really into that.
b) Maybe one or two if I really try.
c) I'm practically a walking cat pun generator.
d) I have so many cat puns; it's purr-plexing!

How many cats do you currently own?

a) None. I prefer to admire them from a distance.
b) One or two. They keep me company.
c) Enough to rival a small animal shelter.
d) I've lost count. There's always room for one more!

What's your preferred method of relaxation?

a) Reading a good book or going for a walk.
b) Watching a cat-themed movie.
c) Snuggling up with my cats and enjoying their company.
d) Getting a massage from my cats as they knead my back or lap.

What is your reaction when you hear a cat meowing outside your window?

a) I ignore it and hope it goes away.
b) I peek out the window to see if it needs help.
c) I rush outside with a can of tuna - someone is hungry!
d) I meow back in an attempt to have a conversation.

How many cat-themed mugs do you own?

a) None. I prefer my coffee without whiskers.
b) Just one. It adds a touch of feline charm to my mornings.
c) A whole cabinet full of them. Every sip is a purrfect delight.
d) My cats have their own designated mugs. They're part of the family!

How do you react when someone says they're not a cat person?

a) I respect their preference and move on.
b) I try to convince them that cats are amazing.
c) I launch into a passionate speech about the wonders of cats.
d) I bring out my photo album filled with cat pictures as evidence.

How often do you talk to your cat?

a) Only when necessary, like when it's time for food.
b) Occasionally, when I'm feeling extra chatty.
c) Constantly. I share all my thoughts and secrets with my furry friend.
d) My cat and I have full-blown conversations. We understand each other.

How many cat toys are scattered around your house?

a) None. My place is a cat toy-free zone.
b) Just a few. I like to keep them entertained.
c) Toys are everywhere! My home is a feline amusement park.
d) My cats have more toys than they could possibly play with.

Where should a litter box go?

a) Anywhere I don't have to look at it.
b) In the laundry or bathroom.
c) It's not where it's placed but how many you have: at least 2 per cat!
d) I have specially designed furniture in which litter boxes can be placed.

How many cat-related songs do you know?
a) None. Cats and music don't mix for me.
b) Maybe one or two catchy tunes.
c) I have a playlist dedicated entirely to cat-inspired melodies.
d) I compose my own cat-themed symphonies. Meow-sic is my passion!

How often do you find yourself thinking about cats during the day?
a) Rarely. I have other things on my mind.
b) Occasionally.
c) Constantly. Cats are my muse, my inspiration, my everything.
d) I can't think about anything else. Cats consume my every waking moment.

What percentage of your furniture is covered in cat hair?

a) None, and I like it that way!
b) There is the occasional cat hair to be found.
c) Over 60%, but it's ok! We have half a dozen lint rollers on hand!
d) It. Is. Everywhere.

What is your reaction when someone says they're allergic to cats?

a) I sympathize with their unfortunate situation.
b) I offer them a tissue and try to avoid triggering their allergies.
c) I step back - I KNOW how much cat hair is on my clothes!
d) Sadly, I will have to consider ending this relationship.

How many times have you dressed up your cat in a costume?

a) Never.
b) Once or twice for a special occasion.
c) They have a wardrobe that rivals a Hollywood star's.
d) I have a full-on fashion show with my cat every day.

How often do you use the phrase "meow" in your everyday conversations?

a) Never. I prefer to stick to human languages.
b) Occasionally, as a playful expression.
c) I sprinkle "meows" throughout my sentences like a feline language aficionado.
d) I've fully embraced the meow language. It's how I communicate with the world.

What happens to your cat when you go on holiday?

a) I let someone else deal with that.
b) I have a friend bring them food once a day.
c) They stay in a cattery, even for short trips.
d) They have their own dedicated pet sitter who is a trained chef, medic, and tummy rubber.

How many cat-related books do you have on your bookshelf?

a) None. I prefer other genres.
b) A couple of cat-themed books for light reading.
c) My bookshelf is overflowing with cat care guides, cat memoirs, and cat poetry.
d) My cat has its own section in the library. We're working on publishing their autobiography.

What do you wear for Halloween?

a) Something scary, like a ghost costume!
b) I slip on a pair of cute cat ears. Meow!
c) I go big: cat ears, tail, face paint, furry paws, collar – the lot!
d) My cats and I coordinate our outfits to match a theme. This year, we are going as characters from the Wizard of Oz.

Have you ever entered a cat competition?

a) No?
b) I once submitted my cat's photo to a 'cutest cat' competition!
c) My cat attends in-person cat competitions.
d) As we speak, I am working on their resume for President of the USA.

How many cat-themed calendars do you own?

a) None. I stick to digital calendars.
b) Just one. It's a nice way to keep track.
c) I have multiple cat calendars at home and work.
d) I have a custom-made calendar featuring my cats as the models.

Where should cats sleep at night?

a) The floor seems comfortable enough.
b) In a fluffy cat bed.
c) In bed with me. They get prime position.
d) Cats decide when and where they sleep – we are merely vessels that aid them in this key feline act.

How many cat-related YouTube channels do you subscribe to?

a) None. YouTube is not my go-to platform.
b) Maybe one or two channels for occasional cat videos.
c) I'm subscribed to at least five cat channels.
d) I have my own cat YouTube channel. My cats are internet sensations!

You spot a cat-themed item in a store! Do you buy it?

a) Not really my thing, to be honest.
b) I consider it; it IS cute!
c) I immediately add it to my shopping cart. I can't resist the cat charm!
d) I buy it without hesitation, even if it means clearing out the store's entire stock.

What's your reaction when you see a cat sleeping in a funny position?

a) I smile and appreciate the cuteness.
b) I snap a quick picture to share with friends.
c) I burst into uncontrollable laughter and struggle to catch my breath.
d) I take it as a sign of the cat's attempt to communicate with aliens.

How often do you visit cat adoption websites?

a) Never. I prefer not to browse.
b) Occasionally, just to see the adorable faces looking for homes.
c) I've donated to them in the past.
d) It's the first place I go when I want a new cat!

What's your reaction when you spot a cat-shaped cloud in the sky?
a) I appreciate it for a moment and move on.
b) I point it out to others, saying, "Look, a cat!"
c) I take it as a divine sign and make a wish for more cats in my life.
d) I grab my camera and start an Instagram account dedicated to cloud cats.

When was the last time you went to the toilet on your own?
a) ... what?
b) Most of the time, I'm fine and can sneak into the bathroom without my cat following me.
c) I can't remember when one of my cats didn't come with me. Maybe six months ago?
d) Why would I want to go to the bathroom on my own? The more cats with me, the merrier!

What is your biggest cat-related renovation project?

a) There are cat-related reno projects?
b) I put in a cat door!
c) We built indoor walkways and shelves for our cats.
d) A large catio so my cats can have indoor-outdoor access while always being safe.

How often do you rearrange your schedule to accommodate your cat's needs?

a) Rarely. My cat adapts to my routine.
b) If it's necessary for their well-being.
c) I prioritize my cat's needs above everything else. Their wish is my command.
d) My cat and I have synchronized schedules. We are a purrfect team.

Now, add up all the different As, Bs, Cs, and Ds you answered to find out IF you are a Crazy Cat Lady!

If you answered mostly A...

Cats just aren't your thing, and that's ok! We all have flaws. It's not that you dislike cats; it's just that you appreciate other animals just as much. You're happy to go a whole day without thinking about cats, and you might not even have a single cat photo or meme saved to your phone.

There is just one thing, however...

Somehow, you've ended up with a Crazy Cat Lady book, and this doesn't happen merely by chance. Either someone in your life sees traits you are missing, or you subconsciously picked up this book knowing that enlightenment was only a few pages away. We encourage you to keep reading; you might just find your own brand of crazy by the end of the book!

If you answered mostly B...

You definitely have your Crazy Cat Lady training wheels, and you're happy to flaunt them to the world! You're curious about cats and love what they add to your household, and there is a growing sense that you're not quite complete without a cat in your life.

You've recently upped your game when it comes to talking about cats, interacting with cats, and learning all the appropriate cat meows and yips. Keep up the hard work! Your cats AND friends have already started noticing the difference!

If you answered mostly C...

You are a seasoned pro. You know you're crazy about cats and have the evidence to back it up. It may have started as a small obsession, but it has snowballed into something spe-cat-ular and beautiful.

You adore your own cat(s) and celebrate the way this love has infiltrated other areas of your life. You've developed your own special crazy cat lady style that feels natural and authentic – this isn't something you do but who you are. You likely mentor less experienced Crazy Cat Ladies toward their fullest potential.

If you answered mostly D...

... and then there were cats!

Life didn't truly begin for you until cats entered your life, and now they are your entire world. You speak, eat, walk, and dream cat, and your craziness is celebrated across the web.

You refuse to be bound by such illogical chains as common sense, financial constraints, or balanced opinions. You celebrate cats in increasingly creative and slightly unhinged ways, making you a true role model to cat lovers around the world.

Keep up the good work!

Part 2: What KIND of Crazy Cat Lady are you?

Crazy Cat Ladies, like the enigmatic world of cats themselves, come in various shapes and sizes, each with their own peculiar feline flair. These individuals defy conventional norms, proudly embracing their profound love for cats with a mix of humor, eccentricity, and undeniable passion.

Our second quiz looks more specifically at what KIND of Crazy Cat Lady you may be, as Harry (Quality Control) believes there are some important distinctions. A quick look first at some well-known cat lovers from history and their cats' vital role in their lives.

Empress of the Cats: Empress Matilda (1102-1167)
Empress Matilda, a remarkable figure from the 12th century, was renowned for her fierce loyalty to her feline companions. She often preferred the company of her beloved cats to that of the human courtiers, earning her the title "Empress of the Cats."

Matilda's feline obsession reached such heights that her cats were said to have worn golden collars and dined at tables fit for royalty. The Empress Matilda's legacy exemplifies how a passion for cats can elevate one's status to regal heights.

The Reclusive Healer: Florence Nightingale (1820-1910)
Known as the founder of modern nursing, Florence Nightingale led a life dedicated to caring for the sick and wounded. Yet, amidst her life's noble mission, she shared an unusual connection with cats. Florence Nightingale's cats were her devoted companions, and it is believed that she had over 60 cats across her lifetime.

She believed cats had a soothing and healing presence, and her home was filled with feline friends. The "Reclusive Healer" shows us that even the most revered figures in history had their own unique cat-loving quirks.

The Literary Maven: Mark Twain (1835-1910)

Not all Crazy Cat Ladies are women! Mark Twain, the celebrated author of "The Adventures of Huckleberry Finn" and "The Adventures of Tom Sawyer," was not only a master of the written word but also a fervent cat enthusiast. He famously stated, "If man could be crossed with a cat, it would improve man but deteriorate the cat." Twain's home was a haven for cats, often hosting up to 19 at a time.

His connection with felines transcended the literary world, earning him the moniker of "The Literary Maven," proving that great minds and cat adoration go hand in paw.

The Feline Feminist: Shirley Jackson (1916-1965)

Shirley Jackson, the Iconic author of "The Haunting of Hill House" and "The Lottery," left an indelible mark on the world of literature. She was an unapologetic advocate for feminism, and her love for cats was a celebrated part of her identity. Jackson's cats were her confidants, and her house was a sanctuary for strays.

As a writer who defied societal norms, she is rightfully known as "The Feline Feminist," using her literary talents to promote the idea that cats, like women, deserve respect and autonomy.

The Cat Comedian: Phyllis Diller (1917-2012)

Phyllis Diller, the iconic stand-up comedian, was known for her outlandish humor and her larger-than-life persona. She shared her home with an array of cats, each with a distinct personality and comedic potential.

With a life full of laughter and laughter-loving cats, Phyllis Diller embraced her role as "The Cat Comedian." She demonstrated that cats can be the best audience and even better punchlines.

Now, onto the next quiz, which will determine what KIND of crazy cat lady you are!

Each question will have four possible answers. Circle the one that fits you best, then add up how many of each letter you scored.

What does your ideal Saturday look like?
a) Spending quality time with my cats.
b) Shopping for cat-themed merchandise.
c) Reading books about cat behavior.
d) Treating my cats to a spa day.

Your cat knocks a glass off the table. Your reaction is:
a) Comfort and console the cat.
b) Make a mental note to buy a cat-themed coaster.
c) Analyze the cat's behavior for signs of stress.
d) Laugh and say, "Cats will be cats!"

What's your go-to conversation topic?
a) My cats' antics.
b) My latest cat-themed find.
c) Cat psychology and behavior.
d) How amazing my cats are.

How many cat-themed items do you own?
a) None; nothing compares to my cats.
b) If there is a cat on it, I probably own it.
c) Only items that are relevant to the care of my cat.
d) Me? None. My cat, however, has their own wardrobe.

What's your favorite cat-related hobby?
a) Cuddling with my cats.
b) Scouring antique shops for cat figurines.
c) Watching cat behavior YouTube videos.
d) Whatever makes my cat the happiest.

Your ideal vacation destination is:
a) Anywhere my cats can come along.
b) A place known for its cat-related souvenirs and activities.
c) Visiting a cat sanctuary in another country.
d) Cat cafes around the world.

Your cats have their own Instagram account:

a) No, that's a bit much.
b) Yes, and it's filled with cat-themed accessories.
c) Yes, and it's all about cat education.
d) Yes, and they're basically celebrities (in my mind, at least!)

How many cat-related books have you read?

a) None – I'm more interested in MY cats.
b) I tend to collect pretty notebooks with cat covers more than I read cat books.
c) A small library's worth.
d) Only a couple - I prefer to create photo books of my cats.

Your dream job would involve:
a) Working from home with your cats.
b) Managing a cat-themed store.
c) Conducting cat behavior research.
d) Owning a cat spa and café.

How many cat-related documentaries have you watched?
a) None, although I have video clips of my cats being cute on my phone. Would you like to see one?
b) A couple, but they are not a priority.
c) I've seen them all.
d) Only ones related to how to treat your cat like the goddess she is.

Your cats have a dedicated room in your house:
a) No, but they're allowed anywhere.
b) Yes, and it's a cat-themed wonderland.
c) Yes, it's designed for their comfort.
d) Yes, and it's nicer than my own room.

When you meet a fellow cat lover, what's your first question?
a) "How many cats do you have?"
b) "Do you collect cat figurines?"
c) "Do you know about feline body language?"
d) "Do you treat your cats like royalty, too?"

Your ideal date night with your significant other involves:

a) Staying in with your cats.
b) Visiting a cat café.
c) Attending a lecture on cat health.
d) Planning a surprise cat-themed evening.

What's the first thing you do when you wake up?

a) Say good morning to your cats – they're likely on the bed with you.
b) Change out of your cat-themed PJs.
c) Study my cat's reactions to ensure they are well this morning.
d) Serve your cat their breakfast before you make your own.

Your cats have inspired you to:

a) Enjoy the simple pleasure of their company.
b) Buy a significant amount of cat-themed stationery.
c) Become as knowledgeable as possible in feline behavior.
d) Pamper them like the feline royalty they are.

What's your favorite cat-related pickup line?

a) "Are you a cat? Because you've got me feline fine."
b) "Is your name Catnip? Because you're irresistible."
c) "Are you a veterinarian? Because I'm feline love with you."
d) "Is your heart a litter box? Because I've got some love to deposit."

What's your cat's role in your daily routine?

a) Assistant chef during breakfast.
b) Personal stylist for your cat-themed outfits.
c) Co-presenter in your cat behavior YouTube channel.
d) Chief executive officer of your cat-dominated household.

Your cat brings you a "gift" (read: a toy mouse) while you're on a work video call. Your response is:
a) Thank them graciously and give them some cuddles.
b) Proudly display it to those on the video call.
c) Analyze the behavior behind their "gift-giving."
d) Introduce your cat as your new business partner.

What's your cat's title in your will?
a) Chief Beneficiary.
b) Custodian of the Cat Collection.
c) Co-Executor of the Estate.
d) Supreme Ruler of Inheritance.

What's your favorite type of gift to buy your cat?
a) Cat-themed dishes.
b) Lots of small toys filled with catnip.
c) Cat puzzle and IQ games.
d) Sparkly collars and fluffy beds.

When you see a cat meme, what's your typical reaction?

a) Chuckle and share it with your friends.
b) Print out the best ones and post them on your fridge.
c) Analyze the humor from the feline perspective.
d) Think that your cat could have pulled off the meme better.

Your cat wakes you up at 3 a.m. by knocking things off the nightstand. Your response is:

a) Give your cat some attention and try to go back to sleep.
b) Curse the cat-themed alarm clock on the nightstand – it got in your cat's way!
c) Analyze your cat's behavior for stress signs.
d) Get up to play with your cat – they clearly need you.

How do you celebrate your cat's birthday?
a) With extra treats and cuddles.
b) By throwing a cat-themed birthday party.
c) By researching cat-friendly cake recipes.
d) By planning an elaborate cat birthday photoshoot.

Your cat scratches the furniture. Your reaction is:
a) Redirect them to a scratching post.
b) Consider buying furniture covers.
c) Research cat behavior modification techniques.
d) Embrace it as a cat-inspired design choice. You're never going to win this battle.

Your cat's vet bills are:

a) Reasonable and within budget.
b) Significant due to health accessories.
c) High due to regular check-ups and preventive care.
d) A non-issue. Your cat has top-notch insurance.

What's your favorite feline fashion statement?

a) A cozy cat-themed sweater.
b) Cat-shaped sunglasses.
c) A collar with a built-in GPS tracker.
d) A matching outfit with your cat.

What's your favorite genre of literature?
a) Cat mysteries featuring feline detectives.
b) Fiction where cats have secret societies and save the world.
c) Non-fiction cat behavior manuals.
d) Cat poetry, of course. I dabble in it myself!

You're redecorating your home. What's the primary color scheme?
a) Tuxedo cat black and white.
b) Shades of tabby brown and calico orange.
c) Analytical gray with accents of litter-box blue.
d) Cat-eye green with a fur-textured rug.

Now, add up all the different As, Bs, Cs, and Ds you answered to find out what kind of Crazy Cat Lady you would be!

If you answered mostly A...

You cannot imagine anything more purrfect than an afternoon spent with your cats. You're not particularly fussed about cat accessories or memes, not when you have your own fluffy bundles of joy to cuddle up with.

There is an almost psychic link between you and your cat(s): you understand all their wants and needs, and they tolerate you in a way they do no one else. The attention and love you show them are returned in full, and they value the quality time you have together almost as much as you do.

Sure, sometimes you might re-arrange the rest of your life around your cats, but that's simply because you prefer their company – sorry, not sorry!

If you answered mostly B...

Like the Egyptian Pharaohs whose worship of cats followed them even in death, you collect into one place everything cat-esque. Cute figurines of cats? Irresistible. Stationery sets covered in paws and whiskered faces? You have them in multiple different colors and binding types. Cat shirts and hats with built-in kitty ears? Please, you have dedicated space in your wardrobe for cat-related clothes.

You know what you like, and there is always a shelf or nook at home to place any newfound treasure. To be frank, you have no choice BUT to keep buying more cat objects as someone keeps mysteriously knocking them off the shelves...

If you answered mostly C...

You are a cat intellectual – a cat-llectual if you will! You have a Ph.D. in cat body language, a Master's in nutrition, and an Archaeology Diploma specializing in kitty litter.

You know cats, and it is what makes you such a fantastic cat mum. You need to know precisely what will help your cats live to their fullest potential, and you're prepared to put the work in to find out.

You've read all the books, watched all the YouTube videos, and put into practice all the tips and tricks you've learned. Your cat(s) couldn't be more grateful.

If you answered mostly D...
All hail the Queen!

Your cat is the emp-purr-ess of the household, and you wouldn't have it any other way. Whatever they want, they get – and often with a side serving of salmon and kitty treats.

Your cats contribute so much joy and happiness to your life that you have rightfully placed them on a pedestal, and it is likely topped with a velvet cushion.

No expense is too great; no time spent on them ever misplaced. The value they bring far outweighs any potential financial cost.

Bonus Crazy Cat Lady Type!

This book largely celebrates the joyful silliness of being a Crazy Cat Lady. However, there is one additional type of Crazy Cat Lady that often underpins all other versions: The Advocate (or, as we say in Crazy Cat Lady language: the Advocat). Rather than place The Advocate in with all the other options, this page is dedicated to the hard work that cat lovers often put in at home and into the wider cat community. In the list below, circle all the forms of cat advocacy YOU practice:

[adoption] [working at a shelter] [speaking out about animal rights] [caring for colony cats] [challenging legislation] [anti-declaw] [rescue] [cat rights] [TNR (Trap-Neuter-Return)] [cat education] [fundraising] [feeding strays] [volunteering] [rehabilitation] [raising awareness] [challenging beliefs] [fostering] [outreach] [donating] [no-kill] [SPCA]

Thank you for all you do! If you want to become more involved in advocacy, you can call your local pet shelter or see what others are doing online. There are always many opportunities to get involved!

Part 3: What TYPE of cat would you be?

Let's be honest. We've all thought about what it would be like actually to be a cat at some point, right? Maybe you have envisioned napping all day in a warm sun patch or delighted in the thought of someone ELSE doing all the cooking and cleaning. Let's turn this up a notch and put a little bit more of the crazy back into the Crazy Cat Lady title, and see which type of cat we would be if someone could wave a magic wand and grant us this one wish...

Each question will have four possible answers. Circle the one that fits you best, then add up how many of each letter you scored.

What is your ideal way to spend a rainy day?

a) Sleeping in.
b) Staying indoors, keeping an eye on everything.
c) Playing board games.
d) Watching a movie with a friend.

How do you react when someone rings your doorbell unexpectedly?

a) Don't bother getting up; they can let themselves in.
b) Hide and observe from a distance – maybe they'll go away if they don't see you.
c) Pounce to the door, curious to see who it is.
d) Hope it's a friendly face!

What is your response to a loud noise outside your window?

a) Keep snoozing. It's probably nothing.
b) Perk up and stay on high alert.
c) Investigate and try to get a better view.
d) Look to a family member for reassurance.

You see a new box in the house; what's your first (not exactly human) instinct?

a) Wouldn't that be lovely to take a nap in?
b) Check it in a curious yet vaguely suspicious manner. It may be a bomb! Or a pirate ship!
c) Jump in immediately. It's a new playground!
d) Wait until someone shares it with you.

What is your reaction when you hear a can opener in the kitchen?

a) Yawn and go back to sleep.
b) Stay where you are, but keep a watchful eye. Someone may be cooking!
c) Race to the kitchen with hopeful eyes.
d) Follow your housemate closely, expecting a share of their meal.

If you were a cat and your human was sitting on the couch with a blanket, you would...

a) Join them and take a nap.
b) Watch from a distance, assessing the situation.
c) Leap onto the back of the couch and start a game.
d) Snuggle up next to them, demanding attention.

How do you feel about exploring the great outdoors?

a) No thanks, I'm perfectly content indoors.
b) Cautiously, and only during the day.
c) Absolutely, I love climbing trees and exploring high places.
d) As long as my favorite human is there to explore with me.

A new piece of furniture is in your territory, and your cat instincts come out. How do you react?

a) Claim it as your new resting spot.
b) You don't like change and wish you had kept the old one.
c) Use it as a launching pad for fun antics.
d) Sit on it and wait for company.

You're invited on a car trip!
a) Absolutely not. Let's stay home instead.
b) Only if it's absolutely necessary and in a car with seatbelts. Safety first.
c) Excited! I love the adventure of car rides.
d) As long as we go on this trip together!

Imagine you are a cat! Your human brings home a new stuffed toy. What do you do?
a) Nap on it, claiming it as your own.
b) Approach cautiously and give it a sniff.
c) Bat it around and pounce on it playfully.
d) Ignore it. Real cuddles are better.

How do you feel about sharing your food with others?

a) It's mine, all mine!
b) As long as they keep their distance (and have their own fork), it's fine.
c) I'll share, but only if we can play afterward.
d) Sharing food is a bonding experience.

How do you respond to thunderstorms?

a) Sleep through them; they don't bother me.
b) Hide under the bed until it's over.
c) Sit by a window to watch the lightning.
d) Snuggle up with someone for comfort.

How do you react when you spot a bug crawling in the house?

a) Ignore it. Bugs are beneath me.
b) Keep your distance, but watch it closely.
c) Hunt it down with relentless energy.
d) Alert someone else, hoping they'll take care of it.

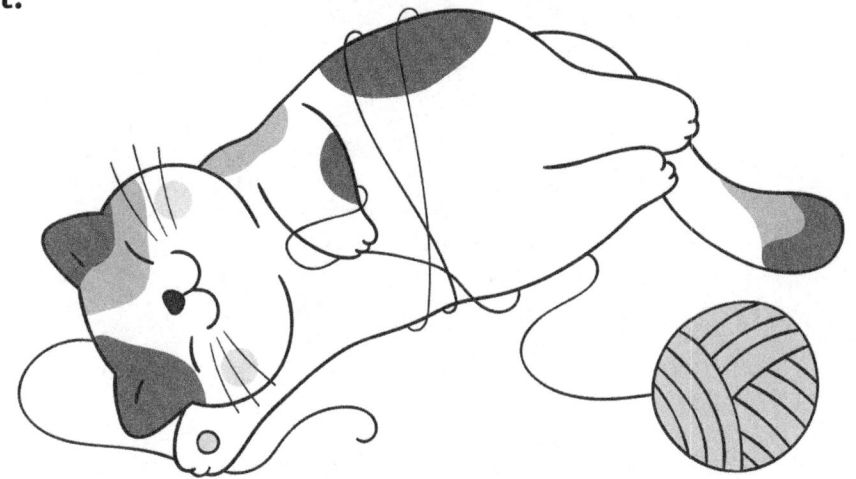

What's your preferred sleeping position?

a) Curled up in a ball.
b) With one eye open, always alert.
c) Sprawled out, taking up as much space as possible.
d) Sleeping with (or on) someone, of course!

It's time for an Instagram photo! You...
a) Strike a lazy pose and look adorable.
b) Side-eye the photographer suspiciously.
c) Attempt a gravity-defying leap for the camera.
d) Snuggle closer and ham it up for the camera.

Friends and family turn up for a party at your house! How do you socialize?
a) Make a brief appearance and then retreat to your room.
b) Greet them, but then keep your distance.
c) Dance! You're more interested in having fun than the people themselves.
d) Become the life of the party.

Oh no! There is a mouse in the house! What do you do?

a) Eh, it will find its own way out.
b) Watch suspiciously as it moves from place to place.
c) Set up an elaborate trap.
d) Decide that this is DEFINITELY a two-person job.

It's the weekend! How do you plan on spending it?

a) Relaxing at home.
b) Watching a murder mystery movie.
c) Hiking! Or cycling! Or rock climbing!
d) Eating out with friends.

The sun is out for the first time in weeks! You...

a) Find a nice warm sun trap to laze in.
b) Pile on the sunscreen, hat, and shades.
c) Head outdoors.
d) A family picnic sounds great!

Cat powers activate! Which of these skills would you rather have?

a) The ability to fall asleep anywhere, at any time.
b) An analytic (and slightly suspicious) mind.
c) Strong climbing and exploring skills.
d) The softest, most cuddly fur in existence.

Now, add up all the different As, Bs, Cs, and Ds you answered to find out what kind of cat you would be!

If you answered mostly A...

Con-cat-ulations! When it comes to napping, you are an absolute star! You don't have the time or energy for the fast-paced life that other cats pursue. Instead, you would rather spend your time finding the perfect sun spot to sleep in. You might be a little lazy, but at least you are comfortable!

There is something incredibly charming about how you can fall asleep almost anywhere, although it does leave you open to people playing with your paws when they think you are sleeping...

Even when you are awake (and it does occasionally happen, not necessarily by design), you are not known for your high energy or strong socialization skills. Instead, you have one or two people you adore who understand your need for quiet time, and you reward them with the softest of hugs. Naturally, you also dominate any sleeping spaces at night - this IS your domain, after all!

If you answered mostly B...

Someone has to be the cautious brains of this operation, and that role tends to fall to you. You're a little anxious, a little suspicious, and a little jumpy when it comes to new things (loud things, weird things, all things). Maybe you're once bitten, twice shy, or purr-haps you've always been a little anxious about the world in general.

The reality is, however, that NO-ONE really knows if there are spiders, pirates, or a sea monster in that box. And, just because the mailman was friendly on those 30 other occasions he's come to the door doesn't mean he hasn't been possessed this time. You take care with everything you see and experience, but this never stops you from loving the people in your life to the fullest extent, even if it means overcoming an array of fears and concerns on a daily basis.

They are worth it - and so are you.

If you answered mostly C...

Some cats can be a bit mousy, but not you! You love adventure, exploring the outdoors, and climbing to the highest places you possibly can. The absolute best thing about being a cat is being able to do all the fun stuff that only cats can do, and the thought of scaling a tall tree and sitting up amongst the leaves feels like a dream come true - at least until you find something else even more cat-tastic to do!

You like humans and other cats well enough, but you don't want them to be passive people in your life. You want to be able to play with them, travel out in the wild with them, and be well-supported in your life of freedom and fun. If they get in the way of that, you're happy to ignore all their instructions and demands to do your own thing. You're confident, a bit independent, and probably the only thing that can distract you from a fun day out is the distant sound of a tin opening...

If you answered mostly D...

Welcome to the couch, Supreme Cuddler and Snuggler Extraordinaire! You love nothing more than spending time with your human(s), especially if it involves cuddling, snuggling, and receiving love. Your purr is musical; your head bumps are gentle and sweet. You wrap around your loved one's legs as though you haven't a single bone in your body, and have we mentioned how soft your fur is yet?

There is a reason why it is almost impossible not to stop and pat you until you fall into a blissful sleep. You even let people touch your paws and rub your belly (don't worry, we won't tell the other cats)!

You might get a little anxious when the people you love aren't close; their safety is important to you, and you can't think of any good reason why they would leave the house at all each day. Still, this is often forgiven when they share your favorite snack with you.

If you answered a mix...

This isn't really a surprise, is it? Cat personalities can sometimes change like the weather, and you are someone who has lots of different priorities.

Some days, you find the purrfect place to nap, and not even the tantalizing smell of freshly cooked chicken from the kitchen can move you from your gentle slumber. On other days, you might feel a little bit jumpy and suspicious and not quite know why (it is not your fault; of course, this is something that has been done TO you).

You might even have days where you want to be outside one minute and back inside cuddling the next, creating an exhausting loop for your owner that you find endlessly (and not so secretly) amusing.

You are a cat of many colors: a tabby of traits, desires, and needs.

Part 4: What does YOUR cat say about you?

So far, YOU have been able to decide how to answer each of the questions, drawing on your deep well of Crazy Cat Lady-like antics, beliefs, and spending habits. However, in Crazy Cat Lady tradition, the tables are about to be turned and the power handed back to the true experts in this field – our cats. Science (as conducted by our Lead Researcher, Spotti Dotti) has demonstrated that the cats we have can say a lot about our personality. Let's put that theory to the test!

Below are 16 types of cats, with their owner's characteristics listed beneath each one.

If you don't currently have a cat, you can reflect on previous cats or the types of cats you are drawn to. Being a Crazy Cat Lover isn't about ownership, after all. It is about passion.

What does YOUR cat say about you?

Tortoiseshell Cat Owners:

Tortie personalities are as vivid and contrasting as their coat, and so is yours! You can shift between different emotions depending on what is happening around you and adapt well to new situations that would leave others flat-pawed. People tend to see themselves in you (or at least a shade or two), making you relatable and easy to talk to.

Persian Cat Owners:

Persian cats are the regal aristocrats of the cat world – they know their worth and are comfortable in their own fur. Relaxed and laid back, their owners are likely to reflect the quieter characteristics of their beloved pet. While a Persian owner may still enjoy time with others, they truly value quiet time alone with a good book.

Tuxedo Cat Owners:
Tuxedo cats may always be dressed for the occasion, but so much more lies beneath that elegant fur. Known for their (often very selective) intelligence, playfulness, and a healthy dose of charm, their owners are easygoing and friendly, with a keen insight and intuition that can sometimes surprise people. Like a Tuxedo cat, it is easy to see their owners in black and white and not notice the depth inside.

Manx Cat Owners:
Manx cats are playful, loving, and just a little bit wild! Their owners share these essential qualities, enjoying time with others and going on adventures. They are also likely to be easy-going and make friends easily – and not simply because that is the easiest way for both cats AND owners to get treats!

Calico Cat Owners:

No matter their size, Calico cats are overflowing with energy, spunk, and attitude. Their owners are often creative and independent spirits, appreciating diversity and risk-taking. Like their cats, they never shy away from a challenge, ready to take on all comers and fight for what they believe is right. Fiercely loyal and sometimes just a touch aggressive, your friends know you will always have their back — and your cat will always have yours.

Japanese Bobtail Owners:

You have to be quick to keep up with a Japanese Bobtail! Playful and clever, Japanese Bobtail owners are social creatures who are always a joy to be around. You especially enjoy activities that maximize your agility and speed. Only a fool (or, perhaps, a dog lover) would underestimate your strong sense of loyalty and commitment to your loved ones.

Bengal Cat Owners:

Incredibly talkative and clever, Bengal cats bring out the wittiness in their owners. Fantastic to chat with; you are also known for your high levels of energy and willingness to give almost anything a go – and chances are, whatever you try, you're going to be good at it! You might be a little bit of a show-off at times, but people can't help but appreciate your skills and expertise.

Scottish Fold Owners:

The bond between a Scottish Fold cat and their owner is deep and incredibly unique. They adore your quiet affection and gentle nature – you make everyone (including your cat!) feel safe and valued. You can evaluate situations around you quickly and adapt to them, while always trying to do the right thing and support others.

Sphynx Cat Owners:
Just like with a Sphynx cat, appearances can be misleading! You might come across as severe and a little aloof at times; however, this is quite the opposite of who you are at heart. You are incredibly friendly and loving, an extrovert who loves to be with others. You're always ready to go out and have fun, and you rarely run out of energy.

Siamese Cat Owners:
Clever and independent, a Siamese catwalks to the beat of their own drum. Thankfully, their owners are known for their patience, flair, and personal wit – you make a fantastic pair! You can be affectionate to the point of devotion, but only to those who show those same traits in return. You're unlikely to waste your time with people who don't treat you well.

Burmese Cat Owners:

Your Burmese cat has never fully outgrown their mischievousness, and neither have you. You are spirited and stubborn but never malicious – you care too much about others to ever want to hurt them in any way deliberately. Instead, you like to keep others as close as possible, especially those you love.

Maine Coon Cat Owners:

The gentle giants of cats, Maine Coons are family friendly and almost dog-like (heaven forbid!) in their behavior. Their owners are often highly sociable, and it's not rare for them to have more than one pet – it's good that you all get along well with each other! Highly intelligent and loyal, everyone in your circle knows just how dependable and kind you are. You're not a fan of conflict and tend to take on the peacemaker role.

Abyssinian Cat Owners:

The Abyssinian cat: sleek, elegant, and strong. Their owners possess their own quiet strength, able to get their points across in a subtle yet thoughtful manner that still demands attention. You can easily keep yourself amused for hours, but don't shy away from quality interactions with others.

Tabby Cat Owners:

Tabby cats are affectionate and warm, their genuine hearts and friendly nature making them utterly irresistible to cat owners such as yourself. They appreciate that you are friendly and a little bit sassy in a happy-go-lucky way, playful, and always wearing a smile. You look for the best in people and have a positive attitude that people can't help but find infectious.

Part 5: And just for fun, some cat quotes!

Congratulations! You are a bona fide Crazy Cat Lady; wave your flag proudly! You have passed all the strict psychological criteria put before you, and it is time to end with just a touch of silly catnip for the soul:
cat quotes from some of their biggest fans!

"What greater gift than the love of a cat?" — Charles Dickens

"Cats are magical. The more you pet them, the longer you both live." — Unknown

"Cats are a smile waiting to happen." — Unknown

"In ancient times, cats were worshipped as gods; they have not forgotten this." — Terry Pratchett

"Cats choose us; we don't own them." — Kristin Cast

"Time spent with a cat is never wasted." — Colette

"A cat can purr its way out of anything." — Donna McCrohan

"Cats are connoisseurs of comfort." — James Herriot

"A home without a cat is just a house." — Unknown

"Dogs come when they're called; cats take a message and get back to you later." — Mary Bly

"Cats are like music; it's foolish to try to explain their worth to those who don't understand." — Unknown

"The smallest feline is a masterpiece." — Leonardo da Vinci

"The cat is nature's beauty." — French Proverb

"Cats leave paw prints on your heart." — Unknown

"A cat is a puzzle for which there is no solution." — Hazel Nicholson

"Cats have it all: admiration, an endless sleep, and company only when they want it." — Rod McKuen

"Cats are the ultimate narcissists. You can tell this because of all the time they spend on personal grooming." — James Gorman

"Cats are like a fine wine; they get better with age." — Unknown

"As every cat owner knows, nobody owns a cat." — Ellen Perry Berkeley

"The way to get on with a cat is to treat it as an equal — or even better, as the superior it knows itself to be." — Elizabeth Peters

From my cats to yours

love

Dedicated to Grimble

Printed in Great Britain
by Amazon